# *The State Schools of Massachusetts*

KATHERINE ANDERSON

AMERICA
THROUGH TIME®
ADDING COLOR TO AMERICAN HISTORY

*This book is dedicated to my husband, Bruce, and to my parents, Kim and Susan. They are my biggest fans and my strongest supporters.*

America Through Time is an imprint of Fonthill Media LLC
www.through-time.com
office@through-time.com

Published by Arcadia Publishing by arrangement with Fonthill Media LLC
For all general information, please contact Arcadia Publishing:
Telephone: 843-853-2070
Fax: 843-853-0044
E-mail: sales@arcadiapublishing.com
For customer service and orders:
Toll-Free 1-888-313-2665

www.arcadiapublishing.com

First published 2019



ISBN 978-1-63499-156-8



Typeset in 10pt on 13pt Sabon
Printed and bound in England

# *Contents*

# *Acknowledgments*

This book would not have been possible without the help of Stephanie Kraus at Historic New England, Douglas Platt at People Inc., and Cliff McCarthy of the Belchertown Historical Society.

# *Introduction*

> The decade commencing with 1842 shows a simultaneous awakening in Europe and America on behalf of the class styled Idiots.
>
> 1898 Biennial Report of the Private Institution for the Education of the Feeble-Minded Youth

In the early 1600s— in Massachusetts in particular—a rather unique population of person was found to be living amongst families: the so-called "feeble-minded." The feeble-minded weren't feared like the mad—quite to the contrary. They were pitied, often well-tolerated by society, seen as children who would never grow up. Many believed that there was nothing that could be done to improve the capabilities of these "idiots"; it was simply their unfortunate lot in life. In Europe, however, noted educator Edouard Séguin worked with idiots at the Bicêtre asylum and showed that even the most disabled of his students showed improvement.

Before the advent of public institutions for the education of feeble-minded youth, the more fortunate of these children were consigned to private institutions such as Dr. Hervey B. Wilbur's school in Barre, Massachusetts which was established before the state began to experiment with similar institutions. Dr. Wilbur's was the only one of its kind in Massachusetts for the better part of the late nineteenth and early twentieth centuries. In its annual reports, the Private Institution (as it was aptly called) took pride in having been established first though Dr. Samuel Gridley Howe's successes at the Perkins School would soon propel the public sector into the limelight as he too proved that feeble-minded children were indeed capable of learning.

A note on terms: often in this book, labels will be used that are no longer correct when referring to individuals with disabilities. However, this book is a work of history and therefore employs the historically correct terms that were used in the context of the state schools. While these terms will likely be found offensive, they were, at one time, considered scientifically accurate descriptors and are an important part of the story of the state school system. The first time a term is used it will be found in quotations to denote that it is no longer in use.

A patient stands in the window of a Fernald dorm. [*Author's collection*]

*Right:* Portrait of Samuel Gridley Howe. [*Massachusetts Historical Society*]

*Below:* Elm Hill, Private School for the Feeble-Minded in Barre, Massachusetts. [*Mike Minicucci*]

Dorm at Massachusetts School for the Feeble-Minded at Waltham. [*Author's collection*]

Dorm at Walter E. Fernald State School. [*Historic New England*]

# 1

# *The Plight of Simple Simon*

> More than nine-thousand idiots, epileptics, and insane in these United States, destitute of appropriate care and protection ... now abandoned to the most loathsome necessities are subject to the vilest and most outrageous violations.
>
> Dorothea Dix

Children and adults with intellectual disabilities—referred to as "feeble-minded" or "idiotic"—were generally the object of pity and charity, an image of sympathy and helplessness, but at the close of the nineteenth century, a second theory emerged: that feeble-mindedness was caused by possession, similar to mental illness. These were individuals bred of sin who were merely a "mass of flesh ... with no soul" as described by Martin Luther. More often than not, these attitudes of hopelessness bred social policy that provided little more than basic shelter, which later translated into long-term confinement.

Feeble-mindedness was linked to poor moral fiber, the result of a "germ" passed through generations of low-bred individuals with inferior intellect. It was nearly impossible at this time to gain public and political support for the education of these children and many were committed to orphanages or abandoned. Idiocy was transformed into a physical malady, a spreading disease linked to genetics and heredity.

Early institutions were meant to train the inmates in viable skills such as weaving and furniture repair. However, the understanding that the feeble-minded could indeed be educated was slow in coming. Society largely misunderstood the purpose of these training schools; the public expected complete cures in large numbers and when that was not achieved, a movement arose, calling for the expansion of these schools. This was the beginning of the large-scale institutionalization of people with intellectual disabilities in the United States.

The growth of these isolated institutions led to the widespread segregation of the feeble-minded under the guise of protecting them from the world. In 1883, Massachusetts Governor Benjamin Butler wrote, "Give them an asylum ... but not a school. A well-fed, well cared for idiot is a happy creature. An idiot awakened to his condition is a miserable one." In spite of educational successes, it was considered far more humane to quarantine the feeble-minded and keep them warehoused than to educate them, making them aware of their unfortunate status.

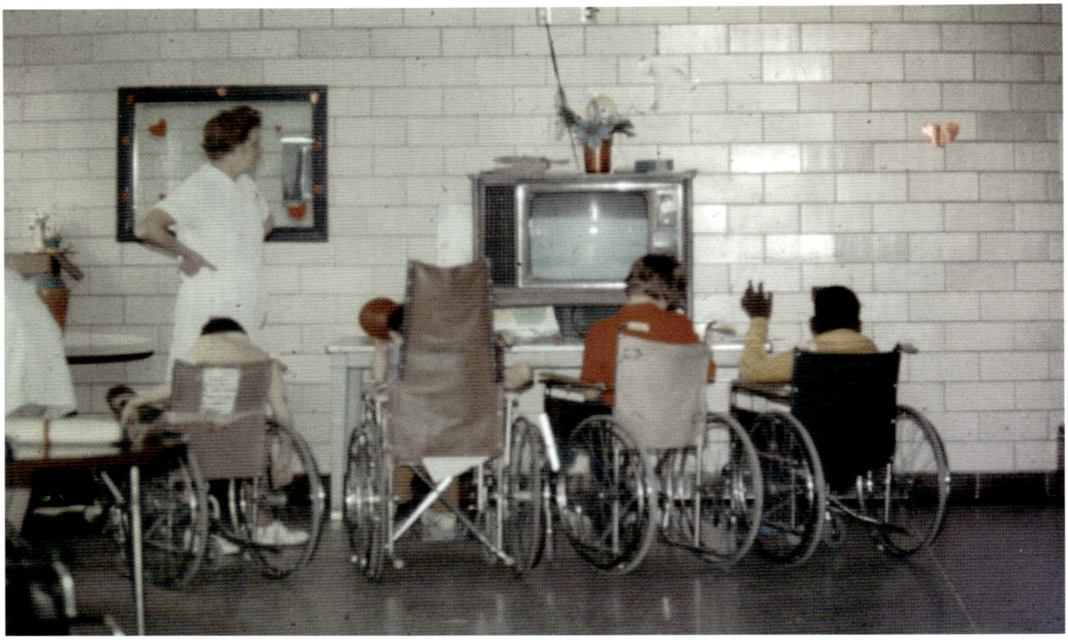

Day room at Walter E. Fernald State School. [*Author's collection*]

Day room at Walter E. Fernald State School. "Some men see things as they are and say, why; I dream things that never were and say, why not." George Bernard Shaw; Robert F. Kennedy. [*Author's collection*]

West Building, Walter E. Fernald State School. [*Historic New England*]

Belchertown State School green. [*National Register of Historic Places*]

The case for confinement was further strengthened by the advent of intelligence testing which was originally developed as a screening mechanism for school children in Paris. In the United States the test was adapted by Dr. Henry H. Goddard, director of research at the Training School for Feeble-Minded Girls and Boys in Vineland, New Jersey. Goddard used the test to separate out "idiots," "imbeciles," and "morons," new labels he had created. He administered the test to as many children as he could and began shuttling them into the training schools. The creator of the test, Alfred Binet, was appalled that it would be used in this way as he believed that intelligence could be increased by good education that was tailored to the individual whereas Goddard believed that intelligence was a fixed entity that could not be altered.

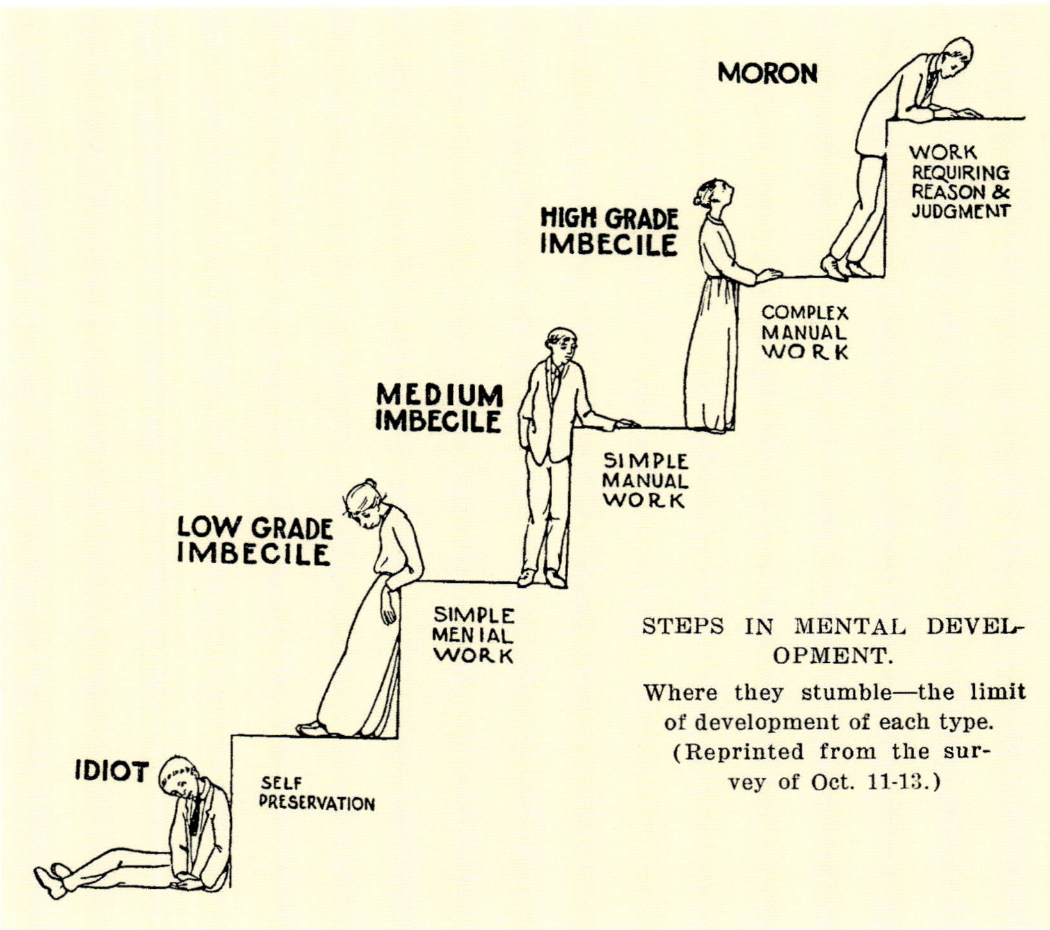


Imbecile scale from Stanford-Binet test of intelligence *circa* 1921. [*Author's collection*]

State school superintendents campaigned heavily against the burdens caused by the feeble-minded, announcing that they were not capable of supporting themselves and would never be more than an immense burden to the public. They also cautioned against allowing the feeble-minded to marry or produce children, referring to them as "tainted" and suggesting that "certain families should become extinct." Much like the fervor that swept 1930s Germany, the "Eugenic Alarm Period" convinced the American public that unless strong measures were taken, these "defectives" — the feeble-minded—would cause "defilement of the race." Laws were enacted making it illegal for them to marry, allowing for medical sterilization and forced segregation to prevent future generations of idiots.

Northwest Building, Walter E. Fernald State School. [*Museum of disABILITY History*]

It was immediately clear that managing these enormous institutions was going to be a challenge. For just shy of a century, both asylums and state schools were governed by the State Board of Insanity, established in 1898. There was no separation between the mentally ill and intellectually disabled. State schools would not be separated from the umbrella of asylums until the creation of the Department of Mental Retardation in 1987. Until that time, state schools were overseen by medical doctors, furthering the suggestion that disability was a disease to be treated in isolation or quarantine.

I Ward and food service building at Wrentham State School. [*National Register of Historic Places*]

# 2

# *The First Schools*

> Nowhere is wisdom more necessary than in the guidance of charitable impulses. Meaning well is only half our duty; thinking right is the other and equally important half.
>
> Samuel Gridley Howe at an 1866 Cornerstone-Laying in Batavia, New York

In January of 1846, the governor of Massachusetts appointed three commissioners, including noted social reformer Samuel Gridley Howe, to "investigate the condition of idiots" in the Commonwealth. The committee was quickly granted permission to take ten children who had been deemed "feeble-minded" and begin educating them in already existing establishments. On October 10, 1848, Howe opened the first public school in the United States for children with intellectual disabilities in a wing of the Perkins Institute for the Blind of which he was director.

The Joint Committee on Public Charitable Institutions visited in March of 1851 and declared that "[Howe's] experiment seems to have succeeded entirely." The Committee suggested the school be given its own location and was moved to a rented space in South Boston. It operated there from 1856 until a permanent location was established in 1887 on a 180-acre parcel overlooking a quiet suburban area in Waltham. The new campus was located near the Waverley Station of the Fitchburg and Massachusetts Central Railroad from which it would take its nickname of the "Waverley Campus."

Perkins School for the Blind. [*Author's collection*]

The first home for the feeble-minded in South Boston. [*Museum of disABILITY History*]

Campus view, Walter E. Fernald State School. [*Author's collection*]

Once in its permanent location, the Massachusetts School for the Feeble Minded flourished under the direction of Superintendent Dr. Walter E. Fernald. On March 6, 1890, the first sixty-one boys and girls were transferred from the custodial wards at South Boston to the Asylum Building at Waverley. By December of 1891 the move was complete, and the South Boston wards emptied completely.

The patients' routines at Waverley consisted of a mix of classroom education, manual and industrial training, and recreational activities that included formal gymnastics classes. A school department with graded classes was opened in 1892 followed by an expansion of the Tufts and Boston University Medical School teaching programs that had been established in 1884. By and large, as the school expanded, it gained and retained national and international stature.

As the first superintendent, Dr. Fernald carried the Massachusetts School for the Feeble-Minded through the first two decades of the twentieth century. Early on in his tenure he brought about a shift in the school's philosophy, reflecting the growing societal fear of increased deviancy, crime, poverty, and immoral behavior, all linked to feeble-mindedness. Annual reports stressed the need to separate male and female patients to prevent them from bearing "defective" children and therefore spreading their feeble-mindedness.

In 1896 the decision was made to increase the patient population from 600 to 1,000 as the mission of the school expanded. Applications to the school had risen by nearly thirty percent as the school began to accept chronic, pauper, delinquent, epileptic, and physically disabled cases that were not considered "trainable" but still needed care.

School building and gym, Walter E. Fernald State School. [*Historic New England*]

Patients engaging in manual training, Walter E. Fernald State School. [*Author's collection*]

Assembly hall, Walter E. Fernald State School. [*Author's collection*]

New administration building, Walter E. Fernald State School *circa* 1993. [*National Register of Historic Places*]

Farm building, Walter E. Fernald State School. [*Historic New England*]

With the rise of the study of Eugenics—from the Greek meaning "well born"—Dr. Fernald advocated strongly for the use of genetics in promoting the survival of the highest quality human beings by eliminating the unfit from the human race. The science had its roots in evolution and in 1901, Sir Francis Galton, cousin to Charles Darwin, proposed that his cousin's theory of "survival of the fittest" could be taken a step further: Galton believed that genetics could be used to engineer a fitter version of humanity in which feeble-mindedness, and by extension low morality, could be bred out. This practice was often referred to as "Social Darwinism," and its tenets took hold in the treatment of those with any kind of intellectual disability.

Dr. Fernald wrote in 1915, "the results of eugenic research are so impressive ... that we are in possession of knowledge which would enable us to markedly diminish the number of feeble-minded persons in a few generations if segregation and surgical sterilization of all known defectives were possible."

Boys' dorm, Walter E. Fernald State School. [*Historic New England*]

Girls' home and south nurses' home, Walter E. Fernald State School. [*Historic New England*]

East Building, Walter E. Fernald State School. [*Historic New England*]

## 3

# *Expansion*

> Our feeble-minded schools are not prisons, but homes in which a useful, happy, rational home life is carried on to the fullest possible extent.
>
> 1911 Trustees Report, Wrentham State School

By the turn of the century, the population of the Massachusetts School for the Feeble-Minded had swelled to 1,000 patients which was considered the "limit for successful operation." The state searched for a second site in Eastern Massachusetts, south of Boston, in order to accommodate the growing number of patients being committed from that area. The Trustees of the Waverley campus purchased a 450-acre parcel in Wrentham for $36,973.

Wrentham was recognized as the Commonwealth's first school to employ a standardized plan for wards and employee housing, plans that would later be adopted by Belchertown State School as well. The school opened officially on April 1, 1910, and 217 new patients were admitted, mainly from the surrounding community, bringing the total population to 239, including boys who had transferred from Waltham.

The Massachusetts School for the Feeble-Minded served as a parent institution throughout Wrentham's early years. The Trustees remarked that the school was "not only helpful to the children themselves, but [was] of benefit to the community". By removing these children from the community, the school was preventing them from living lives of "idleness and ignorance," becoming menaces to the morals of the community.

Wrentham immediately gained a reputation as a leader in the training of feeble-minded youth and would remain so through the mid-twentieth century. Generally, they followed the methods already developed at the Waltham campus, combining study, labor, and recreation, providing highly structured programs and routines. Younger children were educated using the Seguin and Kindergarten methods. The older students were assigned to graded classrooms for academic study and participated in occupational therapy such as weaving and working the farm. There were music, gymnastics, and dance programs in the evenings.

School building, Wrentham State School. [*Museum of disABILITY History*]

Dorm A, Wrentham State School. [*Museum of disABILITY History*]

Old Administration Building, Walter E. Fernald State School. [*Historic New England*]

Marion Moore Building, Wrentham State School. [*National Register of Historic Places*]

Boys' Industrial Building, Wrentham State School. [*National Register of Historic Places*]

Campus Building, Wrentham State School. [*National Register of Historic Places*]

E Building, Wrentham State School. [*National Register of Historic Places*]

Once the population at Wrentham began to climb, the Trustees at Waltham recommended the establishment of a similar institution in the western part of Massachusetts to serve the growing number of admissions from that region. On February 19, 1916, it was announced that the state legislature had voted to purchase more than 800 acres encompassing five family farms in rural Belchertown. The state school farm was established ahead of any new construction; the existing farm buildings were renovated to accommodate the first group of boys that transferred to Belchertown from Wrentham State School.

The town presumed the state school would be a "considerable stimulus to industry and trade," welcoming the addition of jobs and shared resources of which the town might avail itself such as the state school fire station, water supply, and later their telephone switchboard. In addition, the town was pleased to be able to offer programs that would serve the "feeble-minded children of Western Massachusetts who hitherto have been compelled to go to the distant schools at Waverley and Wrentham."

View of farmland, Belchertown State School. [*National Register of Historic Places*]

The architectural firm of Kendall and Taylor—the same firm that designed the campus at Wrentham—was hired to design Belchertown as well, producing a nearly identical cottage plan in the same architectural style. The first buildings constructed were a girls' custodial building and two boys' dormitories, a service building, a storehouse, and two additional employee cottages. Formal opening ceremonies were held on November 15, 1922. George A. MacPherson was appointed superintendent and sixty-five boys were transferred from Fernald in time for opening day. A little over a week later, 128 more boys arrived from both Fernald and Wrentham.

It wouldn't be long before more construction was authorized in order to house the growing population. Along with additional dormitories and employee housing, the state authorized the construction of a Colonial Revival-style administration building that was closely modeled on its predecessor at Wrentham. A proper schoolhouse with a gym and auditorium space was added as well as two boys' dormitories, a carpenters' shop, a superintendent's house, and an off-site water tower. Additional funds were appropriated again in 1928 for the construction of more dormitories and new storage cellars for the farm.

Much like Wrentham and Fernald, Belchertown employed work programs alongside their education programs. It was remarked in the local paper that presumably when the "plant gets fuller under way ... many industries ... will be inaugurated such as carpentry, shopworking ... weaving of carpets and rugs, making of brushes, brooms, and doormats."

F Dorm, Belchertown State School. [*National Register of Historic Places*]

Girls' Industrial Building, Belchertown State School. [*National Register of Historic Places*]

Administration Building, Belchertown State School. [*National Register of Historic Places*]

Superintendent's House, Belchertown State School. [*National Register of Historic Places*]

The children would also work the expansive farm caring for the dairy herd, acres of fruits and vegetables, and, at one point, turkeys. Playgrounds were constructed and sports activities organized. The state school community immediately set to work planning festivities such as plays, movie nights, and country fairs. These events were open to the townspeople and forged a connection that would last for more than two decades.

State school farm exhibition, Belchertown State School. [*New England Small Farm Institute*]

Rear of E and F dorm, Belchertown State School. [*National Register of Historic Places*]

# 4

# *The Era of Prosperity*

> As we look forward to another year of service, we earnestly hope that the plans for rapid and orderly development of the institution may proceed without interruption.
>
> Trustees, Belchertown State School for the Feeble-Minded Annual Report 1923

Throughout the first decades of the twentieth century, all three state schools flourished. In spite of the negative views of feeble-mindedness that formed the basis of each school's philosophy, they continued to provide both training and opportunity for their patients.

Belchertown, as a main example, was a fixture within its community. Most activities on campus were planned with town involvement in mind. An assembly hall inside the main school building doubled as a theater where residents would present plays to which the townspeople were invited. On some evenings and weekends, the staff would show films using the state of the art projection room where residents and townspeople could mingle while watching a double feature. In the canteen, items made by the patients in the school's industrial departments were available for sale to the public.

For the patients, there was a large gymnasium with a bowling alley, a number of playgrounds and basketball courts, and an on-site beauty parlor and barber shop. The farm not only grew all the food needed for the school, it produced enough of a bounty to sell to the townspeople. The school had a prize-winning dairy herd as well as an active piggery. The farm produced hundreds of thousands of quarts of milk, nearly thirty thousand eggs, and tens of thousands of pounds of fruits and vegetables. All three schools employed its patients in a number of occupational roles, especially on the farm, which played a large part in the treatment program.

McPherson Infirmary, Belchertown State School. [*National Register of Historic Places*]

G (Medical) Building, Belchertown State School *circa* 2008. [*Author's image*]

Schoolhouse and Gym, Belchertown State School. [*National Register of Historic Places*]

Manual Training School, Walter E. Fernald State School. [*Historic New England*]

Perhaps due to their more isolated location or maybe in part because of Dr. Fernald's focus on research, Fernald did not report the same level of community engagement as Belchertown. Often the only community outreach noted in the annual reports was in the form of lectures or school visits in which the Fernald staff examined the town's children for feeble-mindedness. Year after year the annual reports for the state school boasted of the strides made in identifying disabilities among children and in raising awareness about the trap of feeble-mindedness.

Fernald did, however, provide a great deal of recreation for the "inmates." In one annual report, the superintendent noted that the "children" (this included the adults that were said to be, in their minds, children who were nearly helpless and would always be so) spent most of their time out of doors playing on the playgrounds that had been installed at each of the residences. He also spoke of how much the children enjoyed music, a piano or organ in each schoolroom and sitting room. Both boys and girls played on baseball teams in the summer and went sledding, skating, and skiing in the winter. There were movie shows every Monday and the staff hosted a dance or party every week.

The farm house, Walter E. Fernald State School. [*Museum of disABILITY History*]

Manual training school exhibit, Walter E. Fernald State School. [*Author's collection*]

Activities center, Walter E. Fernald State School. [*Historic New England*]

Gymnasium, Walter E. Fernald State School circa 2011. [*Author's image*]

All three schools adopted a vacation program— though it was referred to as parole—in which residents would be allowed to go home for a prescribed length of time with staff approval. Some residents had been away from the school for years, checking in only occasionally in order to maintain ties with the staff and other residents.

In 1927, in order to accommodate the growing Belchertown state school, the neighboring poor farm was purchased and added to the state school's acreage. The farm had been running a deficit and the town had previously voted to sell. A closed-door agreement had been made years before, in secret, and the town resented the state school for its underhanded dealings with the state. Superintendent McPherson stepped in to smooth ruffled feathers and the town was mollified.

The state schools were among the largest employers in town and employees were afforded good salaries and advancement opportunities, as well as the option to live on campus in rather comfortable circumstances. The schools reported low turnover rates well into the 1940s and employees who were known to mistreat the patients were terminated immediately. At the peak of its census, Belchertown State School employed nearly 1,500 staff members and administrators. As of 1944, almost half the staff population had worked there for five or more years. All three schools gave clinical demonstrations and conducted school-based clinics. Volunteers supported both the academic and recreational programs at the schools, a practice that is still in place in remaining institutions.

North Building and Boys' Home, Walter E. Fernald State School. [*Historic New England*]

Poor farm, Belchertown, Massachusetts circa 1992; burned 1993. [*National Register of Historic Places*]

Employee cottage #6, Belchertown State School. [*National Register of the Historic Places*]

Employee cottages #8 and 9, Belchertown State School. [*National Register of Historic Places*]

By and large, the direct care staff was devoted to the patients at the state schools. They hosted birthday and holiday parties, purchased gifts for them, and often took them home on weekends or for holidays, giving the patients a break from the campus and a taste of home. They provided round-the-clock care with an average staff ratio of one staff member to every five residents.

West nurses' building, Walter E. Fernald State School. [*Historic New England*]

# 5

# *Signs of Trouble*

> ... society, moved by pity for some special form of suffering, hastens to build up establishments which sometimes increase the very evil which it wishes to lessen.
>
> Samuel Gridley Howe, Keynote Address

In September of 1953, Ben Ricci and his wife, Virginia, committed their first-born son to Belchertown State School, a decision they had not taken lightly but had been the only option for Bobby, who had been diagnosed as retarded. For the first month they were not allowed to visit Bobby, ostensibly to allow him to adjust to his new environment. Once they were finally able to visit, they and the rest of the children's parents were restricted to a waiting room in the dorms and not allowed to wander through their children's living quarters.

Like the other parents who believed the medical staff at Belchertown knew best, Ricci didn't question those kinds of rules and regulations, until he was asked to join the Friends of the Belchertown State School and found that many of the parents had concerns about both the conditions at and the operation of the state school. It was the late 1960s and the patients were still being referred to as "inmates," crowded into the filthy wards with little to no privacy.

It was now left to the Friends to purchase basic items such as toothpaste, soap, and sanitary napkins. The board also purchased televisions for the day halls and took on the responsibility of maintaining them. They sponsored birthday parties and holiday celebrations, which was once the responsibility of the institution. The state no longer funded the purchase of everyday needs such as washcloths and bath towels, never mind Christmas gifts and decorations.

Slowly but surely, in a matter of a few years, one superintendent, backed by one very short-sighted Department of Mental Health, managed to unravel every ounce of goodwill that had been earned by the state school over the last half century of its existence. In October of 1971, Ben Ricci decided to act: it was time to sue the state of Massachusetts.

After interviewing fifteen attorneys, all of whom turned him down, Ben met with Beryl Cohen, a former member of the Massachusetts legislature who believed that Ben had a solid case and was willing to help him draft a complaint. In the end, the complaint

G (Medical) Building, Belchertown State School. [*National Register of Historic Places*]

Patient bed, hospital building, Belchertown State School. [*Author's image*]

Examination table, G (Medical) Building, Belchertown State School. [*Author's image*]

Clock in day room of dorm building, Belchertown State School. [*Author's image*]

Swings between E and F Dorm, Belchertown State School. [*Author's image*]

Theater floor, School Building, Belchertown State School. [*Author's image*]

Furniture stamp, Belchertown State School. [*Author's image*]

was forty-two pages long, citing various findings such as raw sewage backing up in the buildings; pest infestations; shortage of staff; even an absence of seats on the toilets. There were no partitions in the bathrooms. Showers were a communal affair, not unlike those in a prison, and the buildings themselves were deemed unsanitary.

Once filed, things moved quickly. The first judge assigned to the case, ninety-six-year-old Francis J. W. Ford, issued a restraining order that froze all admissions and prohibited the transfer of any patient to a facility for the mentally ill, which had become a common retaliatory practice. Concurrently, similar practices were in place at Fernald, where parents were also discouraged from visiting their children for the first month of their commitment, ostensibly in order to allow them to adjust to their new surroundings.

In 1971, James Shanks, a staff reporter for the *Springfield Republican*, published the first in a series of scathing articles entitled "The Tragedy of Belchertown" in which he shared with the public the abhorrent conditions found at the state school. Accompanied by images taken by staff photographer Vincent D'Addario, the series gave the general public its first glimpse inside the institution that was now embroiled in a very public lawsuit.

Infirmary cupola, Belchertown State School. [*Author's image*]

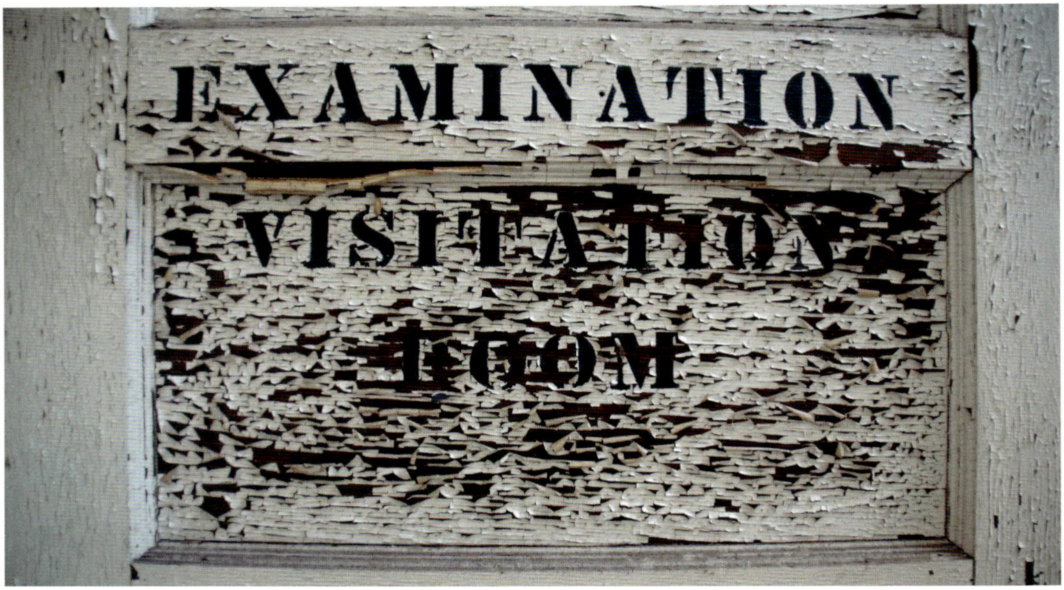


Dorm sign, Belchertown State School. [*Author's image*]

Schoolhouse and Gym, Belchertown State School. [*Author's collection*]

The first building, K Building, was demolished in 1977, followed by A Building two years later. Both embodied the infamous "back ward" where patients were isolated and neglected. Agricultural activities at Belchertown State School ceased in 1972. The farm staff was either dismissed or reassigned to other employment on the main campus, primarily in the maintenance department. The buildings that once served the farm were eventually adapted to other uses and the management of the fields themselves was assumed by UMASS.

State School Farm, Belchertown State School. [*National Register of Historic Places*]

State School Farm, Belchertown State School. [*National Register of Historic Places*]

Schoolhouse theater, Belchertown State School. [*Author's collection*]

Poor farm, Belchertown, Massachusetts. [*National Register of Historic Places*]

By 1989, Department of Mental Retardation Commissioner Mary McCarthy announced that the state school would be phased down until it was ready to close completely. The projected date for closure was sometime in December of 1992, nearly thirty years after reaching its highest recorded patient census. Most were overjoyed that the "house of horrors" would finally be dismantled.

The shame of it would be felt personally by the town's residents. They too, they would come to believe, had been complicit, and their need to expunge that shame would contribute in no small way to the reformation and, ultimately, closure of the school.

On the heels of the *Ricci vs. Greenblatt* case that ultimately closed Belchertown, a class action suit was filed on behalf of the patients at Fernald, as well as a number of other state institutions. *Ricci v. Okin* sought to remediate the conditions at Fernald. The resulting provisions took effect in 1993 and provided "a guaranteed level of care, regardless of cost, to compensate for decades of neglect and abuse."

Administration Building, Walter E. Fernald State School. [*Author's image*]

Wheelchair, Walter E. Fernald State School. [*Author's image*]

In the early 1990s, it was revealed that the Fernald State School had participated in highly controversial research studies involving nuclear medicine. Over a period of seven years, beginning in 1946, students were encouraged to join a "Science Club" which promised them extra food, parties, and trips to Boston Red Sox games. The boys were then fed iron-enriched cereals and calcium-enriched milk that contained radioactive tracers that allowed scientists to track absorption. Other participants were injected with radioisotopes of iron.

Northwest Building, Walter E. Fernald State School. [*Historic New England*]

Walter E. Fernald State School. [*Author's collection*]

# 6

# *Surplus Property*

This is a historic occasion, a day we have looked forward to for many, many years.
Ben Ricci on the closing of Belchertown State School

Belchertown was the first of the three state schools to close. Though the closure was announced on March 8, 1989, the official closing ceremony would not take place for another three years. On December 31, 1992, the final three patients boarded a van and left the state school for good. The assembled crowd, including Dr. Ben Ricci, watched as the main administration building was locked for the last time and the keys handed over to representatives from the Department of Capital Asset Management, the agency responsible for managing surplus state properties.

The campus was left largely vacant with the exception of a few buildings that were being used as temporary elementary schools for the town. Another building had already been repurposed as a senior center and the Belchertown Police Department now occupies the back entrance to the state school campus. The Tadgell Nursery first served as an elementary school, then as the western region headquarters of the Massachusetts Emergency Management Agency.

A reuse committee formed in 1979 as the town anticipated the eventual sizing down and potential closure of the school. In 1991, shortly before the official closure of the state school, the Commonwealth of Massachusetts suggested converting the main campus into a medium security prison. Though the town agreed that it was a viable option, they ultimately passed in favor of moving away from institutional development on that site.

Schoolhouse, Belchertown State School. [*Author's image*]

Merry-Go-Round outside D Dorm, Belchertown State School. [*Author's image*]

E Dorm, Belchertown State School. [*National Register of Historic Places*]

Cafeteria, Belchertown State School. [*Author's image*]

Schoolhouse classroom hallway, Belchertown State School. [*Author's image*]

Instead, the site remained vacant. The Belchertown Economic Development and Industrial Corporation was formed along with the Industrial Development Finance Authority in order to push for redevelopment. Much like the Board of Trade, these two boards promised a twenty-year tax break for anyone willing to develop the campus.

While development stalled on the main campus, the New England Small Farm Institute leased a portion of the remaining farm acreage. They in turn leased smaller parcels to local farmers who continued to farm the land. NESFI also established the Belchertown Community Gardens and hosts the town's 4-H club. NESFI continues to occupy the farm as well as the Jepson House while the original barns remain vacant.

Cafeteria, Belchertown State School. [*Author's image*]

Dorm, Belchertown State School. [*Author's image*]

*Right:* Farm silos, Belchertown State School. [*Author's image*]

*Below:* Offices of New England Small Farm Institute, Jepson House, Belchertown State School. [*National Register of Historic Places*]

The main campus was divided into two parcels. Parcel A included the buildings now being used as the police station, senior center, public access television, and more. Two of the three buildings that were leased to the town as elementary schools are now also abandoned. The remaining parcel, Parcel B, is the largest at 156 acres and contains thirty buildings.

*Above:* Melamine plate in storehouse, Belchertown State School. [*Author's image*]

*Left:* Spoon in Administration Building, Belchertown State School. [*Author's image*]

Another development proposal was suggested in 2000 when a resident, Elizabeth Taras, suggested that Belchertown harken back to its brief history as a tourist center in the 1800s by creating a massive resort and spa. The plan was accepted and unveiled to the town in 2005. Shortly after, the town issued a request for proposals, of which twenty-three were submitted. Bridgeland Development of Chicago was chosen as master developer. Construction was set to begin in the fall of 2007 with an anticipated completion date in the spring of 2009. The project stalled before it even got off the ground.

*Above left:* Dorm hallway, Belchertown State School. [*Author's image*]

*Above right:* Basketball in Administration Building, Belchertown State School. [*Author's image*]

The town waited well into fall of 2007 only to have the check from Bridgeland bounce. Bridgeland president Paul McDermott had failed to secure adequate financing for the Belchertown project and the BEDIC terminated the contract; once again the future of the campus was left in the hands of the town. It remained vacant until 2015 when MassDevelopment stepped in with a mixed-use proposal that would demolish the entire campus except for the Administration Building and the buildings belonging to town Parcel A.

*Above:* Wheelchair in dorm, Belchertown State School. [*Author's image*]

*Below:* Children's stuffed toy on steps of storehouse, Belchertown State School. [*Author's image*]

One of the largest remaining buildings was the school house and gymnasium, also referred to as the auditorium. This building once held the classrooms, two gyms, the bowling alley, and an open theater space where movies, plays, and religious services were held. It was flanked on either side by the boys' and girl's industrial buildings. To the left rear of the school house was Dorm M (male), a brick structure in the shape of a cross. To the right rear, slightly farther back than the male dorm was Dorm D (female) at the corner of Elm Street leading deeper into the campus.

*Right:* Schoolhouse and Gym, Belchertown State School. [*Author's image*]

*Below:* Schoolhouse assembly room and theater, Belchertown State School. [*Author's image*]

Directly across from Dorms B, C, and D (all female) were employee cottages 1, 2, and 3. These cottages directly faced the dorms on the opposite side of Elm Street. Interspersed between the dorms were wooden benches and pieces of playground equipment. Behind the female dorms is a swath of protected wetlands. At the end of Elm Street was Dorm A, one of the first wards to be demolished along with Dorm K, a men's dorm on the opposite side of the campus.

*Above:* Employee cottage #9, Belchertown State School. [*Author's image*]

*Opposite:* Dorm, Belchertown State School. [*Author's image*]

G Building, also known as the medical building, was the most modern building on campus and overlooked a deep valley that swept down to the state school farm land. Situated on the aptly named Ridge Road, G Building was also one of the largest remaining buildings with its own fenced in play yard where wooden swings still hung, and the remains of a wooden merry-go-round were buried in the overgrowth.

*Above:* Merry-Go-Round outside D Dorm, Belchertown State School. [*Author's image*]

*Opposite:* Chair in G (Medical) Building day room, Belchertown State School. [*Author's image*]

On the far side of the campus, closest to the police station, stood a cluster of buildings that served, at one time or another, tuberculosis patients, ambulatory patients with health issues, and patients who were bedridden with cerebral palsy and other physical disabilities. The Tadgell Nursery is perhaps the best known of the hospital buildings as it was once home to Ruth Sienkiewicz-Mercer, author of *I Raise My Eyes to Say Yes*, a brutal account of her time as a patient at the state school.

A small burial ground on the opposite side of Route 202 was dedicated in 1925 and landscaped in 1938. The graves of patients who had died at Belchertown were marked with numbered cement bricks, much like other state institutions. Burials continued until 1977 when the cemetery fell into disrepair.

Born at the state school, Albert Warner visited the cemetery regularly. His mother, Celia Warner, was buried under her own numbered marker. He was horrified by the condition of the cemetery and the state of the graves, so he organized a restoration project. A monument bearing the names of all the patients buried in the cemetery was erected in 1987 and in 1994 the state of Massachusetts agreed to further memorialize the cemetery. Every grave was identified and properly marked with the patient's name, approximate date of birth, and date of death. The cemetery was renamed in Warner's honor.

Though burials at the Warner Pine Grove Memorial Cemetery had stopped in 1977, Albert and his wife Agnes—also a former patient—were buried alongside Albert's mother, Celia, number 132. In 2018, another former patient and disability rights activist Donald Vitkus was interred alongside his friends. Donald's time at Belchertown State School is immortalized in Ed Orzechowski's *You'll Like It Here: The Story of Donald Vitkus, Belchertown Patient #3394*.

*Opposite above:* Tadgell Infirmary, Belchertown State School. [*National Register of Historic Places*]

*Opposite below:* Hospital Building, Belchertown State School. [*National Register of Historic Places*]

Warner Pine Grove Memorial Cemetery, Belchertown State School. [*National Register of Historic Places*]

Memorial Stone at Warner Pine Grove Memorial Cemetery, Belchertown State School. [*Author's image*]

Grave marker #132, Celia Warner, Belchertown State School. [*Author's image*]

Grave marker Celia Lindsey Warner, Belchertown State School. [*Author's image*]

Governor Mitt Romney announced in 2003 that Fernald would be closed, and the land sold by 2007. In response to Romney's plan, a group of family advocates and state employee unions requested that Judge Tauro resume oversight of the *Ricci v. Okin* case and assist them in saving Fernald from closure. In 2007, Judge Tauro ordered the Department of Mental Retardation (now the Department of Developmental Services) to consider the individual wishes of the residents before closing the facility.

Campus view, Walter E. Fernald State School. [*Author's image*]

Walter E. Fernald State School. [*Author's collection*]

In 2007, newly elected Governor Deval Patrick petitioned the courts to overturn Tauro's ruling, citing the rising costs of maintaining the Fernald property. The appeal stated that equal or better care could be provided in community-based settings. Instead, the campus was scaled back, and buildings were vacated in waves until only the Marquardt Nursing Center remained in operation. The same year as Patrick's appeal, Fernald was featured in a 2007 documentary, *Front Wards, Back Wards* which chronicled the treatment of the disabled in state institutions.

*Above:* Howe Hall, Walter E. Fernald State School. [*Author's image*]

*Below:* Dorm, Walter E. Fernald State School. [*Author's image*]

By 2010, the only buildings operating were the administration building, the Marquardt Nursing Home, and the Green Building, which housed a specialized pool made specifically for sensitive populations, including those with both physical and intellectual disabilities. The powerhouse at the rear of the campus continued to provide heat and electricity for those few remaining buildings.

The Walter E. Fernald Developmental Center remained open until 2014 when the last patients were transferred to community run facilities. The city of Waltham purchased the property from the state for $3.7 million under the condition that the historic buildings be preserved, though there has not yet been any movement towards preservation.

Wrentham Developmental Center remains in operation, though a few of the buildings on the campus are now vacant. Currently under the supervision of the Department of Developmental Services, there are no plans to close Wrentham.

Swimming Pool, Green Building, Walter E. Fernald State School. [*Author's collection*]

Greenhouse sign, Walter E. Fernald State School. [*Author's collection*]

East Building, Walter E. Fernald State School. [*Author's image*]

Hallway, Walter E. Fernald State School. [*Author's image*]

Administration Building, Wrentham State School. [*National Register of Historic Places*]

Day room, Walter E. Fernald State School. [*Author's collection*]

Dorm, Walter E. Fernald State School. [*Author's collection*]

*Above:* Administration Building, Walter E. Fernald State School. [*Author's image*]

*Left:* Chair in dorm building, Walter E. Fernald State School. [*Author's image*]

*Right:* Waverly Hall, Walter E. Fernald State School. [*Author's image*]

*Below:* Schoolhouse and Gym, Belchertown State School. [*Author's image*]

*Above:* Theater curtain, Schoolhouse, Belchertown State School. [*Author's image*]

*Left:* Open theater doors, Belchertown State School. [*Author's image*]

*Above left:* Balcony seating, Schoolhouse, Belchertown State School. [*Author's image*]

*Above right:* Balcony entry, Belchertown State School. [*Author's image*]

Steps to Schoolhouse and Gym, Belchertown State School. [*Author's image*]

Administration Building, Belchertown State School. [*Author's image*]

*Above:* McPherson Infirmary, Belchertown State School. [*Author's image*]

*Right:* Porch, Hospital Building, Belchertown State School. [*Author's image*]

Burned patient records in dorm building, Belchertown State School. [*Author's image*]

Discarded patient suitcase in storehouse, Belchertown State School. [*Author's image*]

Basketball hoop outside cafeteria, Belchertown State School. [*Author's image*]

*Above:* Discarded paperwork in storehouse, Belchertown State School. [*Author's image*]

*Left:* Halloween decorations in storehouse, Belchertown State School. [*Author's image*]

Egg production records from state school farm, Belchertown State School. [*Author's image*]

Root cellar at state school farm, Belchertown State School. [*Author's image*]

*Above:* Label in classroom of Schoolhouse, Belchertown State School. [*Author's image*]

*Left:* Discarded fan and gurney in hallway of Schoolhouse, Belchertown State School. [*Author's image*]

*Above:* Smoking pavilion outside Tadgell Nursery, Belchertown State School. [*Author's image*]

*Right:* Waverly Hall, Walter E. Fernald State School. [*Author's image*]

Discarded clothing, Walter E. Fernald State School. [*Author's image*]

*Above left:* Discarded shoes, Walter E. Fernald State School. [*Author's image*]

*Above right:* Slide outside dorm, Walter E. Fernald State School. [*Author's image*]

Templeton Farm Colony, Walter E. Fernald State School. [*Author's image*]

Wooden swing, Belchertown State School. [*Author's image*]